I'll Be Here
When You
Need Me

Matt—

I know this has been a hard year on both of us — me losing my Dad and all the trials you've been through. We have become close despite everything. you have become "my" son. I am very proud of you and I know you will do just fine with your new job. Lets make sure we keep in touch with each other. Good luck "my" son and make me proud —

Love you lots —

Mom

Other books by

Blue Mountain Press INC.

Books by Susan Polis Schutz:
Come Into the Mountains, Dear Friend
I Want to Laugh, I Want to Cry
Someone Else to Love
Yours If You Ask
Love, Live and Share
Find Happiness in Everything You Do
Don't Be Afraid to Love
To My Daughter with Love
Take Charge of Your Body
by Susan Polis Schutz and Katherine F. Carson, M.D.

Warmed by Love
by Leonard Nimoy

I'm on the Way to a Brighter Day
by Douglas Richards

Anthologies:
With You There and Me Here
Reach Out for Your Dreams
I Promise You My Love
A Mother's Love
A Friend Forever
You Are Always My Friend
It Isn't Always Easy
My Sister, My Friend
Thoughts of Love
Thoughts of You, My Friend
You Mean So Much to Me
Love Isn't Always Easy
Don't Ever Give Up Your Dreams
When I Think About You, My Friend
I Love You, Dad
I Keep Falling in Love with You
I Will Always Remember You
For You, My Daughter
A Lasting Friendship
I Will Love You
Through Love's Difficult Times
Always Follow Your Dreams
Though We Are Apart, Love Unites Us
Mother, I Love You Forever

I'll Be Here
When You
Need Me

A collection of poems
Edited by Susan Polis Schutz

Blue Mountain Press ™

Boulder, Colorado

Library of Congress Number: 86-72005
ISBN: 0-88396-247-0

The following works have previously appeared in Blue Mountain Arts publications:

"I know that lately," by Susan Polis Schutz. Copyright © Stephen Schutz and Susan Polis Schutz, 1983. "Should you ever find," by Bonnie Bement Golden. Copyright © Blue Mountain Arts, Inc., 1983. "Would it help," by Sheri Carmon; and "I'm one of those people," by Andrew Tawney. Copyright © Blue Mountain Arts, Inc., 1984. "Through Good Times and Bad," by Dawn McCoy. Copyright © Blue Mountain Arts, Inc., 1985. "I Am Here for You" and "I Am Always Here for You," by Susan Polis Schutz. Copyright © Stephen Schutz and Susan Polis Schutz, 1986. "I'll Always Be Here for You," "I'm on Your Side," "Something Is Troubling You . . .," "I Want to Be Your Sunshine," and "I Think the World of You," by Collin McCarty; "I want to tell you that I believe in you," by Joleen K. Fox; and "Only you know what is best," by Terry Everton. Copyright © Blue Mountain Arts, Inc., 1986. All rights reserved.

Thanks to the Blue Mountain Arts creative staff.

ACKNOWLEDGMENTS appear on page 62.

Manufactured in the United States of America
First Printing: October, 1986

Blue Mountain Press ™

P.O. Box 4549, Boulder, Colorado 80306

CONTENTS

Matt —

I'll Always Be Here for You

You and I are friends.

And no matter what else happens
in this crazy world of ours,
I'll always be here for you
in whatever way I can be . . .

to cheer you up,
to keep in touch,
to dry your tears,
to share your smiles,

to care about you
forever.

— Collin McCarty

*love —
your Portland Mom*

I'm on Your Side

I just want to tell you that
I believe you are
one of the best people around,
and someone who,
without a doubt,
    deserves to be happy
        in your pursuits
    and successful in your efforts.

Things don't always go as planned;
    and plans don't always
        work out as soon as they should.
But — because you are the great person
    that you are — I know that your hopes
    will eventually come true for you.

In the meantime . . .
if you ever need
  any cheering up,
all you have to do is let me know.

I'm on your side . . .
  and I always will be.
For every day that I know you,
  my belief in you grows
    a little bit stronger.

— Collin McCarty

Only you know what is best for you,
   but I am here if you need me

You are your own greatest asset —
there is nothing you cannot do.
No one can keep you from dreaming
your dreams, and only you can
prevent them from coming true.
Your achievements are not
determined by your ability alone,
but by the desire you possess
to reach them. There are no
worlds outside of those you
create for yourself, and the only
boundaries are those you establish
and choose to live within.
Never be afraid to defend your
decisions, regardless. No one
can possibly know what is best
for you other than yourself.
And if you ever feel as if you're
losing control, know that I am
here to listen and that I believe
in you.

— Terry Everton

Whenever you need someone . . .

Think of me . . .
when your goals seem
more distant than ever,
for I am always behind you —
cherishing your dreams as my own,
appreciating your struggle to win,
and sharing your pain if you lose.
My love is constant
through your successes
and surrenders,
for it is based on who you are,
and not on how much or how little
you achieve.

Think of me . . .
when you feel alone,
and remember that although
we must sometimes be apart,
we are always close in spirit.
Our lives have become so intertwined
that it is impossible for me to live mine,
without also living a part of yours.

We look at life through the same eyes
and share a bond of understanding
that the miles between us can't weaken —
and a loving closeness
the years ahead won't change.

Think of me . . .
when things go well for you,
for while I'm here to help you
through the rough spots,
just as important —
I want to celebrate your good times,
for nothing pleases me more
than to see your wishes come true.
It always brightens my day
to know yours is going well.

Think of me . . .
and know I am thinking of you.

— Paula Finn

If You Ever Begin to Doubt Yourself, Always Know that I Believe in You

I want to tell you that I believe in you;
I believe in your mind
and all of the dreams, intelligence,
and determination within you.
You can accomplish anything.
You have so much open to you,
so please don't give up on what you want
   from life
or from yourself.
Please don't put away the dreams inside
   of you.
You have the power to make them real.
You have the power to make yourself
   exactly what you want to be.
Believe in yourself the way I do,
   and nothing will be beyond your reach.

— Joleen K. Fox

I'll Be Here When You Need Me

I realize this is a difficult period
in your life;
that you have a lot on your mind,
and you've been under stress . . .

I'm sorry for the times when I responded
    with impatience when what you needed
    was my understanding;
for acting indifferent to your concerns
    when you needed my support;
and for focusing sometimes
    on how little I was getting . . .
rather than on how much I could give.

Please understand that I do appreciate
the difficulties you're experiencing.
I know that you need time to yourself
    to resolve them,
and I intend to stand by you
    through these rough days as readily
as I've shared in your good days.

I don't want to add to the pressures
    you already feel
by demanding more of your time
    and energy than you have to give . . .

So I just want you to know
    that I'll be here
        whenever you want to see me;
and I'll understand
    if you just need to be alone.

— Paula Finn

Would it help
for you to know
how much I believe in you?
When things are hard,
please remember that.
Remember that you have someone
who is always on your side,
walking beside you
whether you win or lose,
whether you're happy or sad.
In the same way that I believe
that a sunny day lies ahead,
I believe in you.

— Sheri Carmon

Always Know that You Are Loved

When life gets you down
and proves once again
that it is unjust,
and when your most precious
dreams won't come true,
I will wish for you
happiness
and rainbow days.
And even though I know
I'm not always able
to cheer you up,
or give you all
the comfort you need,

I love you
as only a true friend can.
You've been in my life
for so long, and I realize
that there is no one else
like you anywhere.

So when you don't feel
like facing the day,
just remember
that you are loved
and that I am here
as a true friend.

— Sheri Daugherty

I Am Here for You
in Every Way

Sometimes we do not feel
    like we want to feel
Sometimes we do not achieve
    what we want to achieve
Sometimes things that happen
    do not make sense
Sometimes life leads us in directions
    that are
beyond our control
It is at these times, most of all
that we need someone
who will quietly understand us
and be there to support us
I want you to know, my friend
that I am here for you
in every way
and remember that though
circumstances in our lives change
our friendship will always
    remain constant
and remember that though
things may be difficult now
tomorrow is a new day

— Susan Polis Schutz

I'm one of those people
who hurts when someone I care about
    is hurting,
and who feels like crying
when someone I'm very close to
    is feeling so sad.
There's nothing I'd like better
than to help you in any way I can —
    to help you heal and feel strong again —
it would make me feel
so much better, too.

Don't feel — don't ever feel — with me
like you're intruding
or asking too much.
I've always been here
to share the good times with you,

and I'm not about to change
my desire
to share with you now.
I'm here for you
in any way I can be.

In smiles or in tears,
in weakness or in strength,
today and tomorrow,
tomorrow and forever,
we'll be there . . .
we'll make it through
together.

— Andrew Tawney

I wish there were something I could
  give you
to make life easier
to assure your decisions to be right ones
to erase the disappointments
to enhance the joys

I wish there were something I could do
  for you
to rebuild your confidence
to provide you with the answers to
  your questions
to guarantee that the future is yours

I wish there were a way that I could
  change the world for you
to make it better
to carve the place where you would like
  to fit in

  But I can only be here for you
    and hope that is enough.

— Donna J. Abate

Something Is Troubling You . . .

The problem that's troubling you now
will disappear . . .
    take my word for it.
But the person it will leave behind
        will be better because of it.

I know that sounds easy for me to say,
but I really believe it; when I look
back at some of the things I've gone
through, I know that they helped me grow.
And that is what a good deal of life
is all about: growing and learning
and knowing that you have more
ability within you than you ever
even dreamed of.

I have a great deal of faith in you.
Not only are you going to make it
through this thing — you are going
to come out of it
stronger and wiser and better
   (if that's possible!)
than you ever were before.

   And if there's anything I can do
      to help out in the process . . .
      all you have to do
            is say so.

                        — Collin McCarty

I know that lately you
have been having problems
and I just want you to know
that you can rely on me
   for anything
you might need
But more important
keep in mind at all times
that you are very capable
of dealing with any complications
that life has to offer
So
do whatever you must
feel whatever you must
and keep in mind at all times
that we all
grow wiser and
become more sensitive and
are able to enjoy life more
after we go through
hard times

— Susan Polis Schutz

No Matter Where Life Leads Us,
    I Will Always Be Nearby

I'm here for you.
No matter what life takes us through.
No matter how many years go by
or where life leads us,
I'll always be nearby.
And if some things in our lives
should change as we get older,
I know our friendship will remain.
Friendships can expand to include
new aspects of a person's life.
We'll keep on growing, but we'll
never outgrow our need for each other —
to laugh together,
to remember how we got through
    the hard times together.
Our loyalty will always be there.
We'll still care.
Sometimes people grow apart,
preoccupied by life's pressures
    and demands.
They simply become too busy
    to keep friendships going.

But not us.
We know that changes will never
    make us strangers.
We can't let go of that wonderful feeling
of being so understood by another person.
I feel so comfortable with you,
and it feels so good to be ourselves,
so natural to talk like good friends talk.
And even if years should go by
    without our seeing each other,
I know that when we meet again,
    we'll smile
as the magic of our mutual understanding
returns to us once more.

— Sharon Leigh Johnson

Should you ever find
some time you'd like to share,
some time when you're alone,
I'm always here,
I'll always care,

and I'm as close
as your telephone.

— Bonnie Bement Golden

I Am Always Here for You

I suspect that
you are thinking about something
that is bothering you
Please share any problems
that you might be having
with someone (it doesn't matter with whom)
because if you just keep these problems
    in your mind
you will not be able to pursue
your thoughts and activities
to your fullest potential
nor will you be able to enjoy
all the great things in life
because problems, whether they are
    large or small
often dominate one's thoughts

You are such a wonderful person
and you should always be happy
and free from nagging worries

I want to remind you that
I am always ready to
listen and understand you
and if you ever need me
I am always here for you

— Susan Polis Schutz

I want to be a comfort in your life . . .

Having you for a friend is such a
comfort in my life,
because I know that I can always come
to you if I need a little help
or if I just need someone to catch
my tears.
I can always depend on you to be
there for me,
to say all the right things,
and to reassure me that everything will
work out just fine for me.
And I truly hope that this is how you
feel towards me,
because of all the people that I know,
you, more than anyone,
deserve to have this same kind of
comfort in your life, too.

— Lisa Carol Brenneman

At Those Times When Life Lets You Down, Remember . . . I'm Here

There comes a time
In all our lives
When it feels as though clouds
Cover even the brightest days,
When the simplest dreams
Seem distant and unattainable.
There comes a time
When days are filled with anger
And nights
With lonely unhappiness.
I know that now
You are experiencing such a time.

If you need someone to talk to —
I'm here.
If you need
Someone to reassure you —
I'm here.
If you need someone
To silently hold you —
I'm here.
And I will always
   be here for you.

— Beth A. Rosenberg

I want to be sensitive to your needs.
When you're tired and overworked,
I want to be able to comfort you
and be your peaceful place in the world.
When something is troubling you,
I want to share my strength with you
and help you solve your problems.
I want to have compassion for your
    frailties,
just as I hope you'll have compassion
    for mine.
I want to encourage you when you tell me
about your successes and your dreams.
And when you need to be alone,
I want to respect your wishes
and give you the time you need.

I know I can't be perfect,
and there will probably be moments
when I don't understand what you need,
but please know that my love for you
is genuine and unchangeable
and that I am always
your faithful friend.

— Donna Levine

You Are Never Alone

Changes are often very painful
to make, even though we believe
that we will eventually be
a happier person
for having made them.
It takes a lot of courage,
faith, and just plain hard work
and perseverance
to change ourselves
and try to work towards goals
that seem so very far away . . .

I sense that you feel
as if you are all alone
and that no one could possibly
know how you feel inside,
or how hard it is some days to
simply make it through the day.
But I think of you daily
and send you my loving.
I feel so many good things for you —
joy, admiration, caring —
and I know that you will
come through it all smiling.

— Carole M. F. Hübel

Always remember this,
   my friend . . .
that between us,
there exists an unwritten
contract that says:

   Count on me;
   confide in me;
   call me anytime.
   My home is yours.
   You are always welcome
      in my life.

                — Anne Gray

I Want to Be Your Sunshine
on a Cloudy Day

I keep thinking
that life will get easier
as we get older,
but somehow
it doesn't seem to
    work that way, does it?

I guess there will always be
difficulties to face,
and trials and tribulations
    trying to get in the way.

They say that experience is
the best teacher . . . I just wish
it wouldn't try to teach us
    quite so often!

Maybe, in time, we'll get
a little better at sorting out
life's problems and dealing with things.
But whether that ever happens or not,
it is — and will always be — a comfort
to know that you and I
      will always be there for one another.

      You'll always be the sunshine
            that gets me through . . . and that's
            what I always want to be for you.

                        — Collin McCarty

I know how much you hurt inside . . .
as if somehow the sun
refuses to shine on you,
while everyone else is still
walking in its warm light.
But in reality,
we all have our sad times,
our pain and loneliness;
these things are not yours alone.

I wish I could put the sun
back in the sky
exactly where you want it;
but all I can do is tell you
that I hurt sometimes, too . . .
and all I can do
   is give you
my hand to hold,
my ears to listen,
   and my heart full of love.

— Donna Levine

If Ever You Need Me . . . I'm Here

If ever the sun brings rainbows to your
    soul, and you want to share —
        I'm here.
If ever success, great or small, is
    yours, and you want to celebrate —
        I'm here.
If ever the change of seasons brings you
    a new start, and you want someone
    to notice —
        I'm here.
If ever the demands and expectations
    of others overwhelm you, and
    you need acceptance —
        I'm here.

If ever sorrow overcomes you,
and you need hope —
I'm here.
If ever storms threaten you,
and you need peace —
I'm here
offering loving understanding
and a place of comfort —
if ever you need.

— Suzanne Sayer

You are so much
like family to me.
We have shared such
beautiful moments of joy,
and we have gone through
such difficult times together,
holding each other up.

I see us as family,
and no matter
where time may lead us,
I will always be there for you,
and I know you will
always be at my side.

— Miranda Moore

Through Good Times and Bad, We'll Make It Together

We seem to spend our lives
planning for the future . . .
tomorrow is always in our thoughts,
while today slips away,
and yesterday sometimes returns
to remind us of our mistakes.
We try to hold the special moments,
forgetting that the best is yet to come;
that tomorrow is another day,
another chance to take,
another dream to fulfill.
Relationships don't always succeed,
friendships sometimes change,
but I want you to know . . .
no matter what else happens to us,
I will always be here for you.
Open arms to hold you,

an open heart to love you,
an open mind to listen.
You will never be alone.
Together we'll create new dreams
and take our chances.
If we fail, we won't hurt so badly,
because a friend's caring love
heals all wounds, no matter
how deep or painful.
So give me a smile that I can return,
a moment that we can share.
Allow me the time
to know you completely,
and I will always love you
just the way you are.

— Dawn McCoy

I can't promise you happiness always. I can't turn all your grey skies to blue. I can't take away your worries and fears or make your dreams come true. All I can do is what I know how to do . . . to love you and let you know that I'll always be here for you.

— Karen St. Pierre

I Think the World of You, and I Know You'll Always Make It Through

I wish I had the right words within me
to encourage you . . . and to tell you
that I know you'll always make it through
   in sunshine or in rain.

You are, without a doubt, one of
the best and most beautiful people
   I will ever know.
And even if my words
   don't always quite say it,
I hope my feelings for you show
that I believe in you . . .
   in your goodness,
   in your strength,

and in your ability to
make the best of every day.

I pray that you will
never stop reaching out for
the aspirations you hope
        to see come true . . .
because I believe in my heart
    that what you dream
            will come
                to you.

— Collin McCarty

ACKNOWLEDGMENTS

We gratefully acknowledge the permission granted by the following authors to reprint their works.

Paula Finn for "Whenever you need someone . . ." and "I'll Be Here When You Need Me." Copyright © Paula Finn, 1986. All rights reserved. Reprinted by permission.

Sheri Daugherty for "Always Know that You Are Loved." Copyright © Sheri Daugherty, 1986. All rights reserved. Reprinted by permission.

Donna J. Abate for "I wish there were something." Copyright © Donna J. Abate, 1986. All rights reserved. Reprinted by permission.

Sharon Leigh Johnson for "No Matter Where Life Leads Us." Copyright © Sharon Leigh Johnson, 1986. All rights reserved. Reprinted by permission.

LisaCarol Brenneman for "I want to be a comfort." Copyright © LisaCarol Brenneman, 1986. All rights reserved. Reprinted by permission.

Beth A. Rosenberg for "At Those Times When Life Lets You Down." Copyright © Beth A. Rosenberg, 1986. All rights reserved. Reprinted by permission.

Donna Levine for "I want to be sensitive" and "I know how much you hurt." Copyright © Donna Levine, 1986. All rights reserved. Reprinted by permission.

Carole M. F. Hübel for "You Are Never Alone." Copyright © Carole M. F. Hübel, 1986. All rights reserved. Reprinted by permission.

Anne Gray for "Always remember this." Copyright © Anne Gray, 1986. All rights reserved. Reprinted by permission.

Suzanne Sayer for "If Ever You Need Me . . . " Copyright © Suzanne Sayer, 1986. All rights reserved. Reprinted by permission.

Miranda Moore for "You are so much like family." Copyright © Miranda Moore, 1986. All rights reserved. Reprinted by permission.

Karen St. Pierre for "I can't promise you." Copyright © Karen St. Pierre, 1986. All rights reserved. Reprinted by permission.

A careful effort has been made to trace the ownership of poems used in this anthology in order to obtain permission to reprint copyrighted materials and to give proper credit to the copyright owners.

If any error or omission has occurred, it is completely inadvertent, and we would like to make corrections in future editions provided that written notice is made to the publisher: BLUE MOUNTAIN PRESS, INC., P.O. Box 4549, Boulder, Colorado 80306.